"A delightful addition to the series. I particularly like the focus on what kids *can* do to handle their anger more constructively, rather than focusing on what *not* to do. . . . Will appeal to kids as well as those who work with them."

—James J. Crist, Ph.D., author of *What to Do When You're Scared and Worried* and *Mad*

"Excellent. . . . Very helpful strategies for helping children deal with anger."

—Marian Marion, Ph.D., professor, Early Childhood Education, Governors State University

Cool Down and Work Through Anger

Cheri J. Meiners, M.Ed.

Illustrated by Meredith Johnson

free spirit
PUBLISHING®

Library of Congress Cataloging-in-Publication Data
Meiners, Cheri J., 1957-
  Cool down and work through anger / Cheri J. Meiners ; illustrated by Meredith Johnson.
    p. cm. — (Learning to get along series)
  ISBN 978-1-57542-346-3
  1. Anger—Juvenile literature. 2. Anger in children—Juvenile literature. I. Johnson, Meredith. II. Title.
  BF723.A4M44 2010
  152.4'7—dc22
                                                                        2009052502

Free Spirit Publishing does not have control over or assume responsibility for author or third-party websites and their content.

Reading Level Grades 1–2; Interest Level Ages 4–8;
Fountas & Pinnell Guided Reading Level I

Edited by Marjorie Lisovskis

10 9 8 7 6 5 4 3 2
Printed in Hong Kong
P17200810

Free Spirit Publishing Inc.
217 Fifth Avenue North, Suite 200
Minneapolis, MN 55401-1299
(612) 338-2068
help4kids@freespirit.com
www.freespirit.com

Dedication

To my grandson Jacob:

May you learn to
express yourself
in calm,
respectful
ways.

Acknowledgments

I wish to thank Meredith Johnson for illuminating the text with her charming portrayal of children. I appreciate Judy Galbraith and the entire Free Spirit family for their dedicated support of the series. I am especially grateful to Margie Lisovskis for her diplomatic style as well as her talented editing, and to Steven Hauge for his guidance on the illustrations and design. I also recognize Mary Jane Weiss, Ph.D., for her expertise and gift in teaching social skills. Lastly, I thank my fantastic family—David, Kara, Luke, Jacob, Erika, James, Daniel, Julia, and Andrea—who are each an inspiration to me.

I like to feel in charge of some things.

2

I might feel sad or frustrated
when things don't go my way,

or when I can't have or do something I want.

Or I might feel hurt
if someone doesn't show respect.

I may feel angry, too.

I might have
a hot face,
tense muscles,
a fast heartbeat,
or loud breathing.

Sometimes I feel like exploding—
with my hands, feet, or mouth!

But hitting, kicking, and using mean words can hurt people and their feelings.
That's not okay.

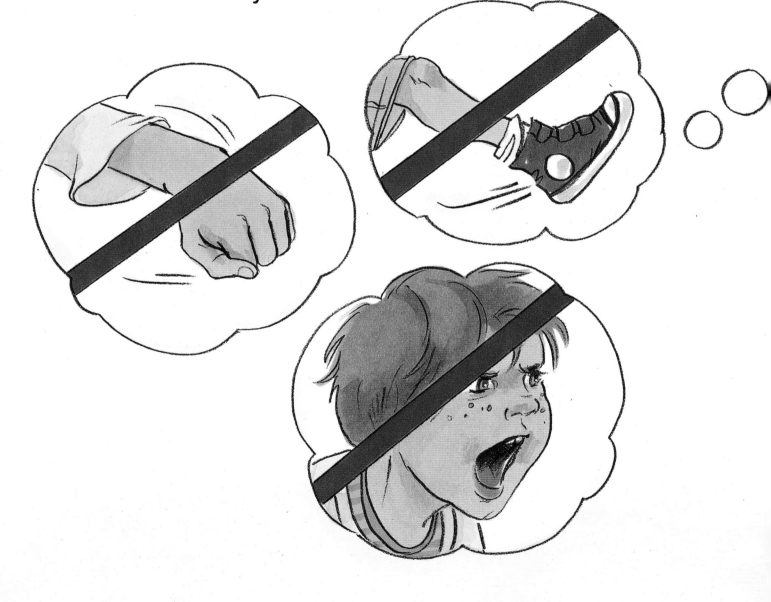

Losing my temper
won't help me or anyone else.
It can cause more anger and hurt.

Keeping my anger shut inside me won't make things better, either.

All of my feelings are okay.
I can admit when I feel angry.

I can learn from my anger,
and find a way to work through it.

First,
I can take some deep breaths
or count to ten to calm down.

I can stop and think
before I say or do something
I may feel sorry about later.

I have lots of ways to cool down.

I might go somewhere quiet
to relax and think.
I can draw or make things,
read a book, or sing a song.

I might also run or play outdoors or spend time with other people.

When I feel calm
I can think more clearly.

I may think about my part in the problem
and what I can change.

Talking things over with somebody I trust
may help me understand
and work through my anger.

I can also talk calmly with the person who was there.

I can show respect as I tell how I feel and what I want.

I can also listen
and try to understand
the other person's view.

When I've been angry
and I've said or done something unkind,
I can say, "I'm sorry."

It won't help to blame anyone else.

I can be patient
and forgive people.

I can remember that everyone makes mistakes sometimes.

When I can't change something,
I can choose to accept it
and make the most of it.

I can look for the best in everyone.

Changing the way I think about someone can change the way I feel.

I can find a way to get along.

When I cool down
and work through my anger,
I can feel peaceful again.

Ways to Reinforce the Ideas in
Cool Down and Work Through Anger

As you read each page spread, ask children:

- What's happening in this picture?

Here are additional questions you might discuss:

Pages 1–11 (understanding anger)

- What does it mean to be in charge of something? What are some things you like to feel in charge of?
- How does it feel when things don't go your way?
- What is respect? *(You might explain respect by saying, "People show respect when they treat others politely and kindly. It is respectful to treat other people the way you would like to be treated.")*
- When is a time you felt angry? What did it feel like?
- What are some things you might feel like doing when you are angry? How can losing your temper hurt someone or hurt the person's feelings? How can it cause more anger?
- Why doesn't it help to keep your anger shut inside you? *(It can lead to health problems like stomachaches or headaches; it can build and lead to more anger or depression; it's harder to get along with people if you don't talk to them and let them know how you feel.)*

Pages 12–19 (processing anger)

- Let's take a big, slow breath, like blowing a balloon up in your tummy. *(Demonstrate inhaling and exhaling slowly. Have children imitate you as you breathe with them.)* How do you feel after taking a big breath?
- What does it mean to calm down or cool down? What are some ways to calm down? *(Discuss "Cool-Down Strategies" on page 33 and other ideas children suggest. Model and briefly practice the techniques with children.)*
- How can it help to think over what happened and what you can do? How can that help you feel less angry?
- Who are some grown-ups you can talk to when you need help?

Pages 20–31 (resolving anger)

- What are ways to show respect as you tell someone how you feel? *(Look at the person. Talk calmly. Talk in a polite tone of voice, and not too loud or too soft. Take time also to listen.)*
- How do you feel when you try to understand another person's view (how someone else is feeling)?
- When is a time you said, "I'm sorry"? How did you feel afterward?
- What does it mean to forgive someone? *(It means that you really feel okay about things now; you don't feel like blaming the person anymore.)*
- In what way can forgiving someone help you? How does it help you get along with the person? How might remembering your own mistakes help you forgive someone else?

- What are some things that you can't change? What does it mean to accept things that you can't change?
- How can changing the way you think about someone help you feel less angry?

Games and Activities for Resolving Anger

Read this book often with your child or group of children. Once children are familiar with the book, refer to it when teachable moments arise involving frustrating situations that may cause anger. Make it a point to notice and comment when children communicate and handle their emotions appropriately. In addition, use the activities on pages 33–35 to reinforce children's understanding of how to recognize, process, and resolve their anger.

Before beginning the games on pages 33–35, make three index-card sets: "Cool-Down Strategies," "Strategies for Working Through Anger," and "Sample Scenarios." Write the ideas below (or similar ideas) on individual cards. Illustrate the cards with drawn, cut-out, or computer-generated pictures. On the back of each card, code the card with a color or number to correspond with the type of card it is (such as blue or the number 1 on "Cool-Down Strategies" cards). Put each card set in a separate bag.

Cool-Down Strategies (18)

- Count to 10, or take big breaths.
- Draw a picture with markers.
- Read this book, or a book you enjoy.
- Take a walk or play a game outside.
- Smile or laugh about it.
- Blow bubbles, or play with water.
- Turn on soft music and move around with a scarf.
- Dim the lights and lie down to rest.
- Sing a favorite song to yourself.
- Do yoga stretches.
- Pretend to be a big balloon. Fill up with air. Then relax and let out the air.
- Give (and get) a hug.
- Walk away until you feel calm.
- Think about a happy time.
- Make something with blocks or paint.
- Swing on a swing.
- Squeeze a Koosh ball or play dough.
- Find a quiet place to think things over.

Strategies for Working Through Anger (10)

- Talk and listen to the person you feel angry with.
- Look at the problem in a different, more helpful way.
- Decide to forget about it and let it go.
- Talk to a friend or an adult you trust.
- Draw a picture or write in a journal.
- Forgive the person.
- Accept that you can't change some things.
- Apologize for getting angry or for your part in the problem.
- Talk to a doll or pet.
- Find a way to make things better.

Sample Scenarios (10)

- Vincent's brother changed the TV channel he was watching.
- Ketty's tower of blocks fell when she put on the top block.
- A girl took a pencil from Omar's desk.
- Erin's younger brother played in her room and broke her favorite toy.
- Some older kids on the playground called Michael names.
- A boy got in front of Zoey in the line for the drinking fountain.
- Dolapo lost at the board game he played with his friends.
- Girls playing jump rope told Raisa that she couldn't play with them.
- A sister borrowed Ben's soccer ball without asking.
- While playing kickball a child kicked Mariah's leg.

Cool-Down Time

Using the "Cool-Down Strategies" cards, have a regularly scheduled "Cool-Down Time" in your day or week. Let a child draw a card to select the activity.

Calming Collages

Materials: Sheets of cardstock or construction paper; markers, crayons, or pencils; magazines; scissors; glue sticks

Directions: Review the "Cool-Down Strategies" on page 33 with children. Then ask them to draw or cut and paste pictures that depict calming strategies. Captions and calming words can also be added. Display the collages. When a child needs help with emotions, refer to the child's collage and ask, "What can you do to calm down?"

Anger Journal

Help children write or draw in a journal as a strategy for understanding and dealing with anger. Here are some prompts you might try, one by one: "Write or draw about something that recently made you feel angry. What did you do?" "Write or draw about what else you can do to solve the problem." "Write or draw what you were thinking about when you felt angry. Then write or draw a different, more helpful way to view the problem."

Stop, Slow Down, and Go

Materials: Index cards and marker; bag to hold the cards; one sheet each of red, green, and yellow construction paper; whiteboard and magnets; 8½" x 11" cardstock (one sheet for each child), folded in half lengthwise; plastic cups with a 2" rim; crayons; craft sticks or straws; tape

Preparation: Make 6–8 "Inappropriate Actions" cards (actions that hurt and don't help) with words or pictures showing ideas such as *kick, yell, bite, punch, lie on the floor and scream, make mean faces, say "I hate you."* Put the cards in a single bag, mixed together with the "Cool-Down Strategies" and "Strategies for Working Through Anger" cards from page 33. Cut a 6"–7" circle from each sheet of construction paper. Use magnets or tape to hang the red, yellow, and green circles vertically on the board so they are arranged as on a traffic light.

Directions

1. Talk about traffic lights and relate them to acting on anger. Point to each circle and say, "We can STOP *(red)* before hurting someone with our body or words. We can SLOW DOWN *(yellow)* and become calm while we decide what to do. We can GO *(green)* by doing helpful things such as talk and listen, forgive someone, and show respect."

2. On the outside of their folded cardstock, have each child make a traffic light by tracing the rim of the cup and then coloring the three circles. Help children tape the stick to the inside bottom and tape the three side edges shut.

3. By turn, have children draw a card and use tape or a magnet to place it next to the appropriate "light" on the whiteboard: red for inappropriate actions, yellow for cool-down strategies, and green for strategies for working through anger. Other children can point to the appropriate color on their own light. When a "red light" card is drawn, have children suggest a strategy they could use when the light turns yellow or green. Children can keep their stoplights as a reminder to stop, calm down, and choose helpful ways to work through anger.

"Be Cool" Card Game

Materials: Index cards and marker

Preparation: On index cards, make "Be Cool" cards with words or pictures showing ideas such as *dance, sing, draw a picture, take a walk, breathe, count to 10, blow bubbles, read a book, talk to an adult, play a game.* Make 4 cards each of 10 activities and one "Hothead" card representing inappropriate display of anger—41 cards in all.

Directions: Discuss the strategies from the cards in terms of how they can help children "be cool" and avoid being a "hothead" while playing a game. Then play the game (it is similar to Old Maid): After all the cards have been dealt equally, children put down matched pairs of cards. Each child in turn lets the person on the left take a card unseen from that child's hand and lay down any matches until all matches are made and one child is holding the "Hothead" card. After the game, children tell why the strategy on their matches is effective or useful.

"Resolving Anger" Cartoons

Materials: White drawing or writing paper, 8½" x 11"; crayons or colored pencils; whiteboard with marker

Preparation: Prepare ahead, or have children prepare, by folding pieces of white paper twice to make four quadrants (frames) when opened. In each frame, draw two stick figures with word balloons.

Directions: Choose a "Sample Scenario" card along with either a "Cool-Down" or a "Working Through Anger" card. On the whiteboard, demonstrate the drawing and writing of a 4-frame cartoon with stick figures that depicts the problem and resolution shown on the cards. Then proceed with Level 1, 2, or 3. (*Note:* The drawings and the words that will be incorporated in the activity are intended as behavioral scripts rather than humorous cartoons.)

Level 1: Let a child draw two cards as in the directions above. Help two children act out a scene based on the cards. Then ask children what you can write in each frame while you complete the cartoon on the whiteboard.

Level 2: Place children in groups of 3–6. Give each group a "Sample Scenario" card along with either a "Cool-Down" or a "Working Through Anger" card. Talk with children about what they can write in the talk balloons. Assist in the writing if needed as children write their own script.

Level 3: Allow children to choose cards and create and "star in" their own cartoon. Let children dictate the script for you to write, if needed. Then have children share their cartoons and discuss their strategies with the group.

Cartoons may then be colored. Compile them in an "If I Feel Angry" book for future discussion or role play.

"Work Through Anger" Role Plays

Level 1: A child draws and is read a scenario card. Ask, "What can this person do to become calm?" Show the child 3–4 "Cool-Down" cards and let the child respond. Then ask, "What can this person do to help solve the problem?" Show a few "Working Through Anger" cards as needed. Fade out the prompt cards when appropriate.

Level 2: A child draws and is read a scenario card. A second child draws a "Cool-Down" and/or a "Working Through Anger" card. Ask, "What can this person do to cool down (or work through anger)?" The children answer the question and then enact the scene using puppets or action figures.

Level 3: Follow the process for Level 2, but this time the two children perform a role play rather than a puppet play. When a strategy prompt is no longer needed, a child draws only a scenario card. Either child tells an appropriate strategy, which they then role-play. Then let children switch roles or choose another scenario.

Free Spirit's Learning to Get Along® Series

Help children learn, understand, and practice basic social and emotional skills. Real-life situations, diversity, and concrete examples make these read-aloud books appropriate for childcare settings, schools, and the home. *Each book: 40 pp., color illust., S/C, 9" x 9", ages 4–8.*

ACCEPT AND VALUE EACH PERSON

Introduces diversity and related concepts: respecting differences, being inclusive, and appreciating people just the way they are.

BE CAREFUL AND STAY SAFE

Teaches children how to avoid potential dangers, ask for help, follow directions, use things carefully, and plan ahead.

BE HONEST AND TELL THE TRUTH

Children learn that being honest in words and actions builds self-confidence and trust, and that telling the truth can take courage and tact.

BE POLITE AND KIND

Introduces children to good manners and gracious behavior including saying "Please," "Thank you," "Excuse me," and "I'm sorry."

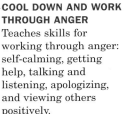

COOL DOWN AND WORK THROUGH ANGER

Teaches skills for working through anger: self-calming, getting help, talking and listening, apologizing, and viewing others positively.

JOIN IN AND PLAY

Teaches the basics of cooperation, getting along, making friends, and being a friend.

KNOW AND FOLLOW RULES

Shows children that following rules can help us stay safe, learn, be fair, get along, and instill a positive sense of pride.

LISTEN AND LEARN

Introduces and explains what listening means, why it's important to listen, and how to listen well.

REACH OUT AND GIVE

Begins with the concept of gratitude; shows children contributing to their community in simple yet meaningful ways.

RESPECT AND TAKE CARE OF THINGS

Children learn to put things where they belong and ask permission to use things. Teaches simple environmental awareness.

SHARE AND TAKE TURNS

Gives reasons to share; describes four ways to share; points out that children can also share their knowledge, creativity, and time.

TALK AND WORK IT OUT

Peaceful conflict resolution is simplified so children can learn to calm down, state the problem, listen, and think of and try solutions.

TRY AND STICK WITH IT

Introduces children to flexibility, stick-to-it-iveness (perseverance), and the benefits of trying something new.

UNDERSTAND AND CARE

Builds empathy in children; guides them to show they care by listening to others and respecting their feelings.

WHEN I FEEL AFRAID

Helps children understand their fears; teaches simple coping skills; encourages children to talk with trusted adults about their fears.

LEARNING TO GET ALONG® SERIES INTERACTIVE SOFTWARE

Children follow along or read on their own, using a special highlight feature to click or hear word definitions. User's Guide included. *For Windows only.*

www.freespirit.com • 800.735.7323

Volume discounts: edsales@freespirit.com
Speakers bureau: speakers@freespirit.com